Augustine: Religion of the Heart

By Dennis E. Groh

Contents

Introduction

Augustine of Hippo (A.D. 354–430) was one of the most important Christian thinkers who ever lived; and he lived in one of the most important ages of Christian history. The significance of Augustine's personal biography is intertwined with the story of his age; both have willed to Christians the perspectives of people living at a truly pivotal time in the West.

Augustine's long life and large body of writings give modern Christians an opportunity to study one of the most influential people in Christian history through-out his development as an adult. We can follow his progress in grace and see how he developed from his twenties to late adulthood.

Augustine's emphasis on the religion of the heart gives him great importance for modern people like us who struggle to understand our place in God's world. No writer of the ancient world so carefully focused on that core of the self, the heart, as we stand before God as Augustine did.

We will encounter Augustine in his loves, fears, combats, and solutions to problems. We will follow him from his birth into a complex home and region, through his gradual conversion to Christianity, and on into his first decade as a Christian. We will see him struggling with his church in the world. Then we will enter into his late adult struggle with doctrines of sin and grace and with his attempts to formulate thoughts about the final peace with God.

Augustine has survived the test of time for Christian readers. Christians in every generation since his death have studied him. Augustine does not draw our contemporary attention because his opinions are timeless or because his views on Christian faith are eternally correct. We continue to read and study him for that indefinable quality of genius that is "able to leap centuries in a single bound," that quality that makes contact with us at our deepest levels of being.

When we read Augustine's works, we recognize his

2

power as a thinker and as a writer. This sense of "literary immediacy" is a human event of the first intellectual magnitude.

And when we begin to laugh and cry at the same things that moved a writer fifteen hundred years ago, we participate in an emotional event of the first importance, the discovery of one of the inns of refreshment on our own long and sometimes lonely journey through life's changing demands and changing responses.

This little book is dedicated to Jeremy and Sara and (lately) Soren who have helped make my journey less lonely.

1

North African Christianity

Augustine was born in the North African town of Thagaste (modern Souk Ahras in Tunisia) in A.D. 354 and died seventy-six years later in 430 in Hippo Regius (modern Bône in Algeria), a city he served as bishop for thirty-five years. This Augustine is often identified as Augustine of Hippo Regius to differentiate him from several other Augustines in the history of the West. I believe this additional identification is unnecessary; none can compare with our Augustine.

As Augustine lay dying on August 28, 430, his episcopal city was besieged by the Vandals led by Gaiseric. The Vandals captured the city and detached it and the entire region from the Roman Empire for the next one hundred years. The West and Augustine's beloved area teetered on the brink of that historical obscurity that passing out of Roman rule often meant. Although his city and his world passed away, the influence of Augustine did not.

Years after Augustine's death, Isidore of Seville, a great collector and commentator on former Christian greats, is said to have written that anyone who claims to have read all Augustine's books is a liar. Augustine wrote no less than 117 books. He became the second most quoted Christian author in the Middle Ages (yielding in frequency only to Paul himself) and the theologian on whose shoulders (or against whose positions) every great theologian of the West has stood.

4

Augustine was a pivotal figure in one of history's pivotal ages. His biography spans one of the most crucial periods in the history of the West. Augustine was born into the period historians call "Late Antiquity" and died in early medieval times. He was born in a world in which Christianity was the officially encouraged religion and died in a world in which Christianity was the only legally permitted religion (since A.D. 399).

Augustine became leader of the Roman Christians of a town as a thirty-seven-year-old priest (A.D. 391) and then as a forty-one-year-old bishop (A.D. 395). But when he died at the age of seventy-six, he was both a bishop of the church and patron and protector of the entire populace of the region. All this activity and responsibility was an amazingly long and important journey for a person to experience in one lifetime.

Theologian of the Heart

We could study the course of this long journey from a number of perspectives, but one aspect claims our attention—what theologian Fred Craddock has called the longest journey any human being can take: "the journey from the head to the heart." Augustine, the heart's theologian, draws our attention, for his long pilgrimage moved from rationalistic and philosophical modes of thinking to the heartfelt and scriptural doctrines of love and grace. As Augustine moved through his life as a clergyperson and theologian, he came to emphasize the importance of his heart's praise, joy, and delight in his Creator's and Savior's mercies.

Augustine did not demean the mind's power to

accomplish many fine things; he never completely abandoned "the head." But Augustine arrived at a position we can properly call "the informed heart." This position evolved as Augustine gained more precision as an interpreter of Scripture and as a clergy servant of a diverse, lively, and difficult people of God. Thus, medieval painters sometimes depicted Augustine holding out his heart in his hands for all to see, inviting us to take the heart's journey with him across the times and seasons of a single, outstanding Christian life.

In the Middle of Things

Augustine's journey started where all our stories start, in the middle of things. He was born into an age, into a region, into a church, into a family, all of whose stories were well in progress when he arrived on the scene.

Augustine was born into the "breadbasket" region of the West. The area's grain fields and olive trees provided great quantities of food for Italy as well as for the heavily populated towns and villages of today's Tunisia, Algeria, and Morocco. The region was divided into a fertile and densely populated coastal region that sported larger cities and towns and a highland plain where both agriculture and village culture thrived. Among the large coastal cities were Carthage (near modern Tunis), where Augustine would study and teach as a young man, and Hippo Regius, where he would live out his ministerial life.

Old Carthage was originally destroyed in 146 B.C. by Rome because Rome feared having a great non-Latin rival in the Mediterranean. But by the beginning of the third century A.D., Carthage had again become the "second city" of the West. In the course of the third century, the secular prominence of Carthage declined while the importance of the Christian church planted there increased. And the bishop of Carthage became, in theory, the leader of the church in all North Africa just as the bishop of Rome was of Italy.

Though a smaller city than Carthage, Hippo Regius was no backwater. The town itself was the second port city of North Africa and was over a thousand years old when Augustine succeeded to the episcopacy there in 395. Augustine could walk crooked and narrow streets whose foundations went back into the remote Punic (Phoenician) foundings of the city and see at the same time the visible monuments of two hundred years of Roman rule. Remains of Roman public baths, market-places, and theaters still dot the North African sites and delight tourists.

In the coastal cities Latin was both the official and the dominant language. The school of Latin speech and rhetoric at Madauros where Augustine studied as a teenager was located in the home town of the legendary Latin writer Lucius Apuleius, author of *The Golden Ass*. The schools at Carthage where Augustine finished his education and began his dramatic rise to fame as a teacher of Latin rhetoric were among the best in the West.

North Africans loved great Latin spoken prose. They were always on the lookout for a great speaker or debate. Thus, when a young ascetic scholar named Augustine came to Hippo Regius in 391 to found a monastery, the congregation of the town grabbed him and forced him to be ordained a priest of their church, although this was much against his will.

In the thirty-nine years of his priesthood, Augustine employed his long study of Latin in both preaching and in public disputations with heretics and with dissenters from the church as well as in great church councils. The people, always swayed by great argument cast by a great speaker, responded favor-ably to Augustine's sermons. Occasionally, he had to reprove his congregation for cheering and clapping too loudly while he preached.

Among the Latinized populace of North Africa, Christianity appeared in 180 for the first time. Significantly, this appearance was in a document titled *The Martyrs of Scilli*. The document sounded a theme of total rejection of the pagan state and its gods.

Within half a generation, North Africa contributed its first (but by no means its last) great Latin theologian, Tertullian of Carthage.

By A.D. 200, Tertullian already had at his disposal some Latin translations of the Scriptures. These Old Latin versions of the Bible held the central place in Christian hearts until Augustine's day. Between 382 and 405, the great church father and biblical scholar Jerome produced the Latin translation of many Scriptures. This translation became the core of the Vulgate, the West's Bible until the Reformation. But Augustine still preferred the Old Latin version of the Old Testament and used North African translations of the New Testament except for the Gospels, which he cited from Jerome's translation.

People of "The Book"

The Bible, especially the Old Testament, was of the greatest importance to North African Christians. They were, above all, a people of "The Book." If North Africans had a natural affinity for Roman law, they had even more appreciation for what they saw to be God's law, the Bible. Tertullian called the New Testament, the clearest proclamation of God's loving covenant with God's people, the new law. That sentiment tended to continue throughout all North African history.

In the middle of the third century, the church in North Africa underwent its worst trials. Empirewide persecutions were aimed at all who dissented from the ways of the old pagan gods. In the wake of those persecutions many entire congregations and many individual members left the church because they had given in to the government's orders to sacrifice to the gods. Many other congregations withdrew from the wider Christian communion, fearing the "pollution" that contact with such flagrant and idolatrous sinners would bring to the church. The bishop of Carthage, Cyprian, was able to pull the church back together but not without enshrining the peculiar

North African custom of requiring rebaptism for those persons who had been converted by the schismatic churches.

People of the Family of God

The Christians of North Africa had a strong sense of being God's family, members of God's household and clan, with all the benefits and responsibilities that these terms imply. North African Christians affirmed that God is the Father and the church is the mother who through baptism brings us to birth as brothers and sisters in Christ. Family language and a deep family feeling saturated North African Christianity.

To the Latin love of family and friendship and the scriptural sense of being God's people was added the notion of kinship. By the middle of the third century, especially in the writings of Cyprian, the "Christian villagers" appear, the inhabitants of the small towns and agricultural villages of the Tunisian and Algerian highlands. By Augustine's day the majority of these villagers were Christian.

By their numbers, their presence, and their deep devotion to religion, these villagers brought to the Christian "family" in North Africa the tight loyalties of the Berber concept of clanship. In a clan world, what is done for or to one person is done for or to every person. A sacrifice made by one member of the group is done for all the people in the clan. When such folks came into the church, they brought their clan loyalties with them.

So, to the long Latin tradition of the importance of the family and to the long tradition of lifelong friendship was added the loyalty to the clan in North African Christianity. This fact meant that highflying notions of being set apart as a people of God often implied (at the ground level) being set against other folks and groups. Thus, controversy and church schism, fueled by deep loyalties to long-dead local saints and to living local heroes, marked the history of North African Christianity.

Augustine shared in the deep family feeling of his fellow North Africans, but he struggled all his days against their combativeness and isolationism. The church of Italy converted him, and Roman literature nourished him. Thus, the vison of a unified African church as a part of the universal church throughout the Roman world claimed Augustine's heart and filled his sermons and writings.

Christian Times

Augustine's vision was all the more important in the light of these new Christian times. Since A.D. 324, Christian emperors had ruled the entire Roman world except for one short lapse under Julian, 361–63. The Empire was fast moving to end the legal status of all religions other than Christianity. The heady oxygen of "one world, one empire, one church" was in the cloudless Mediterranean air.

However, many North Africans preferred their local atmosphere. Their attachments to the Book of Revelation in particular set them firmly against cooperation with this devil-filled world. The images in Revelation of the state's oppression of Christians vividly reminded some North Africans of their own recent deadly-to-unpleasant brushes with Roman government and made them think the Scriptures supported their separatist tendencies. These people were known as Donatists.

Thus, Augustine was born into an ecclesiastical world of two minds, represented by two great separate churches in North Africa: Roman Catholic and Donatist. The "family of humankind" ideal ran head-on into the tribal-clan notion of African church order. With pagan hearts to be won, Augustine considered such a schism to be a scandal, a waste, and a disgrace. But many Donatists were happy. They allowed neither pagans nor Roman Christians to compromise their sectarian purity because the Donatists were convinced these people were going to the same hell anyway.

The Christian Life as Adult Vocation

Such serious choices for and against Christ, for Roman Catholicism or for Donatism, for compromise with the world or for "purity" of withdrawal from the world, demanded an adult level of decision making in Late Antiquity. Thus, the Christianity of that era was a Christianity that tended to encourage people to delay baptism until later in life when they could make their fullest commitment, "putting their hand to the plow" without ever looking back. The church practiced infant and children's baptism; but the church did not romanticize it and did not emphasize such baptism. Fully adult believers' baptism was center stage in Late Antiquity.

Many people in North Africa delayed their baptism until later in life out of fear of backsliding. Many others, like Augustine, delayed baptism until after they had pursued their fortunes and their public careers. The Empire was filled with persons who intended perhaps some day to retire to a life of religion after they had completed their morally questionable dealings with the world and after they had made their fortunes.

We are not surprised then to find a whole generation of great persons who during the middle or late period of their career felt called by Christ. These people simply quit their public offices and jobs and fled to Christ's church. Augustine was one of these people, and his writings give us a wonderful opportunity to study his development as a Christian thinker during what we now know are crucial years in a person's life—the thirties to the sixties.

No contemporary Christian of advanced years, tremblingly presenting himself or herself late in life for Christian baptism or rededication to Christ and not particularly happy about a long and unchristian life stretching behind, need fear Augustine. He was one of us. His life, his regrets, his mistakes, and his loves open to us the gracious possibility of a life lived through all its seasons.

Augustine's knowledge of scriptural Christianity is also a comfort to us. When he converted at age thirty-two, he knew and understood the Scriptures only slightly better than the average literate Christian who has been on the fringes of the Christian church for years.

Augustine's Family of Origin

Augustine's regrets and loves had their origins in the biological family into which he was born. His father, Patricius, was not a Christian. Patricius had thoroughly secular ambitions for his son and brought this ambition to Augustine who rose to prominence through education rather than through public service.

Patricius also brought to Augustine a strong sense of sexuality, not always confined by marital bonds, and a characteristically North African strong temper. The shadow side of the warmth of these North Africans was their impulsiveness and their fits of anger. In North Africa, the anger of God and the fear of mortals before such anger held key places in theological discussions.

So, in addition to sharing his father's ambition (which Augustine's mother also encouraged), the young man also developed his father's temperament. Known as a man of deep loves and loyalties and as a man of hot temper, Augustine was and remained a very sexual man all his life. He was not a womanizer. But from his late teenage years until his conversion, Augustine found life impossible to live without the company of a woman. At the age of nineteen, his long-term (but not last) concubine bore him an illegitimate son named Adeodatus. The name of the boy, meaning "given by god," called to mind not the gracious God of the church but the more somber pagan god of North African religious backgrounds.

Even though Augustine converted to an ascetic style of Christianity at the age of thirty-two and lived all his Christian life as a celibate, he insisted that God never "cures" monks and nuns of their sexuality. For

Augustine, a Christian celibate is a person who has made a decision about how to exercise his or her sexuality, not a person who has passed beyond sexuality.

The Influence of Monica

During all the time Augustine had been pursuing his father's way, another influence hovered around him and threatened to envelope him in her more passive piety. Monica, Augustine's mother, was a devout, strong, and single-minded woman who endured her husband's excesses and shared his ambitions for their son's success. However, she was after their souls for Christ. Monica was relentless in her prayers for Patricius and Augustine and tireless in her efforts to lead them to the church. From her example, Augustine learned how patient and tender (and how relentless) God can be in wooing our hearts. To Monica's single-minded tenderness we owe much of the feminine imagery for God in Augustine's *Confessions* and much of the warmth he brings to the concept of the church as our mother.

If his father is almost invisible in Augustine's great spiritual autobiography, *The Confessions*, Augustine's mother and Augustine's development of his mother's values and love are present everywhere in the work. As Augustine was once a lover of the pagan world and its easy piety, he became a lover of God's church and its piety.

Augustine's formative influences were these: He was born into a family of great ambition, love, and temperament and born into a crossfire of competing values, both in his family and in his world. Thus, the problem of focusing the heart and the will on a single object of devotion preoccupied Augustine all his life. That struggle helped produce the West's greatest theologian.

2

The Pursuer Becomes the Pursued

Augustine was first and foremost a lover. He loved continuously but, like all of us, not always wisely or well. His first love was education. He wanted the best education he could get at the best schools he could afford. By the time of Augustine's baptism in A.D. 387, the pursuit of a great secular liberal arts education had consumed all his early years and much of his parents' resources. Neither he nor his parents minded the sacrifices. Indeed, one of the only warm memories that Augustine had of his father was the way his father scraped and scrimped to send him on for advanced study at the famous school of Carthage.

Augustine never lost that love of "liberal studies," the study of geometry, music, letters, and poetry, though its focus and its content changed throughout his early and middle years. Augustine was later ashamed of his and of his society's values and of the pagan content of much of what he studied. But even at the time when he began to emerge as a mature Christian bishop of the church, around the year 400, he still could not tolerate "half-educated" persons presenting themselves for instruction in church membership.

But Augustine had no trouble with uneducated people. Although one of the best-educated members of one of the most intellectually sophisticated ages in Christian history, Augustine and his contemporaries looked back with love and wonder at the uneducated persons who made up Jesus' circle of disciples. In fact, Augustine and his overly educated contemporaries actually created the myth of the lower-class origins of Jesus' disciples. In reality, the apostles hailed from solidly middle-class backgrounds much like Augustine's family of origin. But the greatly educated minds of Late Antiquity failed to understand this subtle irony.

The Pursuit of Literature

Augustine's first educational love was the study of literature. He spent years at it. And when he came to the apex of his secular career as the professor of rhetoric at the Imperial University of Milan at the relatively young age of thirty, he had become one of the guardians of the classical curriculum. Augustine obtained at Milan what today would be the position of chairperson of a great English department or of a combined studies program that brings together the study of speech, oral interpretation, literature, and philosophy.

Augustine's love of pagan literature, the myths and stories about the gods and the heroines and heroes of literature, was one of his greatest embarrassments later in life. As the mature bishop of Hippo Regius, Augustine castigated himself mercilessly for his past foolishness, such as crying over the tragic love story of the Trojan War and Queen Dido's love for the hero Aeneas. Like many Christians today, the Christian Augustine twisted in shame and pain to remember how he burned with unregenerate sympathy for the ways of the gods, for the heroines, for the easy morals, and for the self-aggrandizing values. But characteristically, Augustine was too hard on himself.

Augustine took his heart to school along with the

rest of him. And, like most truly "serious" people, he loved what he did and did what he loved. In short, he was educable in matters of the heart. The long study of literature was educating his heart, layering his personality, and teaching his heart to rehearse its full vocabulary. Like exercises on the piano, the study of literature equipped him to play all eighty-eight notes on his personality's keyboard. After all, Augustine was both a young "chip off the old block" and a North African full of devotion and capable of deep sympathy.

Looking back on his teenage school days spent away from home in the big city of Carthage, the Christian bishop described himself as a frying pan, a caldron of amorous emotions. Contemporaries remembered him quite differently; they recalled a rather correct and proper young man. But to the inner Augustine, the man who by the year 400 had discovered the disjuncture between the inner person and the outer person (a disjuncture we all live in to some degree), the scope of the meanderings of his heart and the sheer magnitude of its misplaced affections was appalling. Like a modern veteran of Hedonism, what frightened Augustine most was his love of feeling itself. The pointlessness of that love and its ability to shift its focus from one earthly (and hence idolatrous and transitory) object or person to another led him to confess that he loved loving.

The Beginning of the Pursuit of Philosophy

While he was in pursuit of literature, the "philosophers" stormed Augustine's heart. Philosophy became his second love and, as is frequently the case with second loves, he remembered it gently and with enduring affection.

At the age of nineteen, Augustine read a now-lost treatise of Cicero's titled *The Hortensius*. Significantly, philosophy claimed not just Augustine's mind but all of him. Augustine was in the thrall of the promise made by philosophy that he could know the good and love it and by loving it could perform it.

The lure of philosophy to ancient persons was, and is still to people today, the goal of integrated, informed, virtuous living. Philosophy's promise to heal the split in the human self between what we appear to be and what we truly are and to give us harmonious and happy lives claimed Augustine's inner life. Outwardly, his body would move through a great public career as a professor of rhetoric; inwardly, he was an aspiring philosopher.

Years later as a rather embarrassed Christian bishop, Augustine confessed that he had been a lover of secular wisdom and not a lover of Christ, the true and only wisdom of God. However, Augustine never fully repudiated his sojourn among the philosophers, especially those whom Plato influenced; nor would he reject the profit he derived from the writings of Aristotle, whom he discovered at the age of twenty.

Nine Years as a Manichaean

In love with wisdom and in pursuit of a career as well, Augustine (never a man to travel alone) fell in with the Manichaeans. The Manichaeans were a sect (officially outlawed) that blended elements of piety with elements of rationality and science. They combined so-called scientific explanations of the universe with a call to join the struggle to free forces of light from forces of darkness in the universe. The Manichaeans believed that universal struggle to return the creation to its original light and to free it from darkness was enacted in every individual. Thus, individuals were called to live a life of contemplation and ritual practice that would free the light trapped in them.

Manichaeism was a rather inactive view of the ethical life in that individuals were called more to a release than to progress. But these teachings appealed greatly to Augustine because they taught him that the evil deeds we do are not the products of our true nature. The Manichaeans believed these deeds were dictated by an evil force in the universe that was not our true selves.

To an overly educated young man who was struggling with opposing emotions and with a confused self-image, the double appeal of attaining perfect knowledge and perfect virtue while losing one's personal guilt proved almost irresistible. If we could imagine something like a combination of the overly easy explanations of Marxism for what is wrong with the world and the exotic adventurous mythology of the game called *Dungeons and Dragons*, we would come quite close to understanding the appeal Manichaeism had to aristocrats of the West in Late Antiquity. Although Manichaeism was officially outlawed, many of the powerful pagans of the West gave Manichaeism their support.

Precisely the power of Manichaeism to enlist the private loyalties of some of the most powerful pagan aristocrats of the West formed a secondary appeal to Augustine and kept him a Manichaean for almost nine years, even long after he had begun to doubt its teachings. When Augustine tired of teaching students at Carthage, the powerful contacts of the Manichaean "underground" helped him obtain better teaching posts, first at Rome and then at Milan.

At the beginning of his involvement with the Manichaeans, Augustine was attracted by the promise of high intellectual attainment and high ethical demands. Augustine failed on both counts, and he never forgave the Manichaeans for his failure. Manichaean doctrines demanded that he assent to their scientific explanations of Creation and the Fall, that he practice vegetarianism and other ritual behavior, and that he renounce his sexuality if he wanted to join the ranks of the perfect.

Augustine was too smart and too warm a person to be able to do any of these things, so he remained for a number of years in the lower circle of "hearers." He also developed what would turn out to be a permanently bad conscience about his stupidity in joining the Manichaean circle. What seemed at the beginning of his study to be scientific turned ludicrous as he began to observe the world. What seemed to be high ethical demands turned into the passive ethic of freeing the light trapped in each person.

However, Augustine owed the Manichaeans three debts. First, they introduced him to Paul's writings. Paul was enjoying something of a revival of interest among all kinds and varieties of Christian and semi-Christian groups in the West. Second, the Manichaeans prodded Augustine to wrestle with questions involving the origins of human life and human evil. For example, their rejection of the Old Testment pointed him to the Book of Genesis. And third, the Manichaeans cured him forever of trying to duck personal culpability for his own share of responsibility for the evil in the world.

Critics of Augustine's later positions on original sin and grace, so formative in the West, accused him of still being infected by the Manichaean paralysis of moral responsibility and of diminishing the role of human freedom in doing the good. But it was precisely his dislike of the Manichaeans that drove Augustine to try to trace exactly the contours of human freedom and human limitations.

Fright and Flight

Monica, Augustine's mother, was a devout and single-minded Christian who, along with so many other fine women of Late Antiquity, hoped only to bring both her husband and her son to Christian baptism. She suffered greatly over the sinfulness of both and ultimately was a key factor in winning their souls for Christ and for his church. But when her son joined the Manichaeans, Monica received the shock of her life. Despite a reassuring dream that her son would finally be saved, Monica made a frantic appeal for help in rescuing her son. An old Christian bishop wisely advised her to leave the young man alone. The old bishop was operating from the wisdom of personal experience, for he himself had been a Manichaean but had read his way through their unsatisfying books and right out of the sect. Still unconsoled in spite of his reassurance, Monica burst into tearful pleas that the bishop talk to Augustine. Slightly vexed, the bishop said to Monica, "Go away from me now. As you live, it is impossible that the son of such tears should perish!"[1] Monica told Augustine years later that the impatient dismissal was "as if it had sounded forth from heaven."[2]

Some years after his own conversion, Augustine learned to cry for himself. He cried for his former lostness and from his own relief at being found by God. In the midst of the congregation, Augustine heard the parable of the prodigal son; and tears streamed down his face as he remembered all his hardheartedness and all his lostness. But when Augustine was still a young Manichaean, other people had to do his crying for him.

Augustine was in pursuit of the happy life promised by philosophy, and he was fueled by a successful career. Thus, running away became the operating motif of his life as a young man. He ran from his native Thagaste to Carthage; he ran from Carthage and his mother (who had followed him to Carthage) to Rome; and he ran from Rome to Milan. As a wiser middle-aged Christian bishop, Augustine looked back on this flight, which had begun as an attempt to escape grief at his best friend's death, with the gently sorrowful words, "For where could my heart fly to away from my heart? Where could I fly to apart from my own self? Where could I not pursue myself?"[3]

The Pursuer Becomes the Pursued

G. K. Chesterton (English journalist, novelist, poet, and critic) once quipped, "Travel narrows a person." I think he meant that if one travels widely enough, sooner or later one comes to see the common element or the theme that runs through one's own life wherever one goes. In faraway Milan everything caught up with Augustine. He went to church to hear Ambrose, the great bishop of Milan, and to study his style of public speaking. Then Augustine went back again and again to listen to the content.

Ambrose was not only a great preacher; he was also a great interpreter of the Scriptures. For the first time in his life, Augustine listened not only to the literal language and words of Scripture but also to the spiritual and symbolic meanings. Ambrose believed in the "spiritual" exposition of Scripture. People who follow such an approach believe all the words are true but not necessarily literally true. The shock that modern Christians occasionally receive when listening to some trained interpreters of the Scriptures can threaten to shipwreck some modern people's faith. That shock had the opposite effect on Augustine. It saved faith for him.

Augustine had tried a number of times to read the Scriptures but was defeated by what he considered to be the inelegant, commonplace language of the Bible and the unevenness of the advice given. However, in Ambrose's prayful and pious method Augustine saw the central message of the gospel lifted up in both Old and New Testaments. He saw that message as the love of God, the love of self as a child of God, and the love of the neighbor as the self. The long Manichaean parody of the God of the Old Testament as a gross, vicious, and oppressive God and its caricature of the New Testament as a lower form of truth began to fall away from Augustine. God was catching up with him.

Augustine was in his early thirties. Age was catching up with him. He was developing some perspective on his life since he had lived long enough to look back on his existence as well as ahead to something else. Augustine focused his attention on what had eluded him in his long pursuit of education and career, namely, the healing of his own split self.

Like many people, Augustine was filled with the sense that he was changing his own destiny only to return again and again to the same old problem he could not overcome. He had various names for it; but

21

perhaps the best is the name he gave it in *The Confessions*, the problem of two wills. Augustine was struggling unsuccessfully to bring his vision of seeing and desiring the good together with his actions.

As a maturing young man, Augustine began to realize that the problem he was struggling with was not simply a matter of "bad company makes bad morals" or a problem of a nature alien to himself that he could avoid by proper ritual and by proper diet. His own self-made life, his very self, was the problem.

Forces began to converge on the "awakening" Augustine, forces that he saw but whose significance he did not know. The man who had been in pursuit of so many and such opposite things now began to feel pursued. He began to realize that God was seeking him.

Thus, Augustine's long flight from Christianity overtook him. He found himself in Milan in a circle first of philosophers and then in a circle of philosophical Christians. The Christians eagerly listened to and told the latest heroic stories of Christian conversions of the great persons of the Empire: the emperor's advisors, Marius Victorinus (the greatest Platonic professor of Late Antiquity), and Anthony (the Egyptian hermit who achieved not only the vision of God but lifetime chastity as well). Augustine's insignificant pursuit of virtue began to unravel backwards on him as new horizons of virtue began to grow before him.

As his friends and loved ones joined him in and near Milan, Augustine had a growing sense that his life had been pointing toward this moment, that the Truth had been seeking him through all the years when he thought he was seeking truth. The waiting father of the parable of the prodigal son and Augustine's pursuing mother all converged for him in the Roman Catholic Church—in its time-honored authority, in its universal and unruffled confidence in its doctrines, and in its public lifting of the heart toward God and away from the bare facts of nature. Augustine was wavering; he was off-balance. He wanted to cross that threshold to Christian belief but was unable to do so.

Retiring to a little garden in Milan one day during the time of this crucial struggle, Augustine heard the voice of a child, (in Christian circles in Late Antiquity, people thought the voice of a child represented the voice of divine willing). The child was playing a game in a nearby garden; and Augustine heard the invitation, "Take up and read."[4] Remembering how the hermit Anthony had once been so guided to take up the Scriptures and open them for guidance, Augustine turned to the text of Romans 13:13-14 and read, "'Not in rioting and drunkenness, not in chambering and impurities, not in strife and envying; but put you on the Lord Jesus Christ and make not provision for the flesh in its concupiscences.'"[5] Augustine later reported of this moment, "Instantly, in Truth, at the end of this sentence, as if before a peaceful light streaming into my heart, all the shadows fled away."[6]

A man of Augustine's temperament and affections seldom moves by halves and never moves alone. His best friend, Alypius, was nearby; and soon Augustine, Alypius, their friends, and Augustine's illegitmate but beloved son, Adeodatus, were baptized together on Easter, 387. Then, along with Augustine's mother, Monica, they withdrew together to a small country estate in order to pray, to read the Scriptures, and to commune with one another in holy ways.

At that time Augustine thought he was near his journey's end. However, his real journey was only beginning.

[1]From *The Confessions of St. Augustine*, translated by John K. Ryan (Image Books, 1960); Book 3, Chapter 12, Section 21.

[2]From *The Confessions*; 3, 12, 21.

[3]From *The Confessions*; 4, 7, 12.

[4]From *The Confessions*; 8, 12, 29.

[5]From *The Confessions*; 8, 12, 29.

[6]From *The Confessions*; 8, 12, 29.

3

The Sadder but Wiser Christian

As George Bernard Shaw's Major Barbara remarked, "learning something" often feels like "losing something." Feeling that way was Augustine's experience in the ten years after his conversion to Christianity in A.D. 387. When we are in our thirties, many of us still feel we can predict the shape of our lives and the direction in which our loves will take us. However, we often awake in our forties in a far different place than we intended to be and with far different feelings about life than we expected.

Augustine's voyage across this crucial decade was no less stormy and unpredictable than many of ours. And just as we often turn to keeping a diary or personal journal to get our bearings and to measure how much we are changing, Augustine began writing his autobiography, *The Confessions*, in 397 at the age of forty-three.

The Confessions marks a decade of one of the greatest periods of change in Augustine's life; thus, it is different from anything else he ever wrote. For in *The Confessions*, Augustine took inner possession of the life he had been leading in the outer world. This book is as much the story of his heart's journey as it is of his mind's journey and his body's journey. This sharply personal and intimate note sets *The Confessions* off from all other spiritual autobiographies produced in antiquity.

Augustine published *The Confessions* in 400–401 and

apparently did not read it again until he was an older adult. Just a few years before his death, Augustine found a copy and reread it, remarking that he was strangely moved by the book just as he had been moved when he wrote it.

The West has had the same reaction to *The Confessions* as its author had. Even though *The Confessions* was not considered Augustine's most important work in the Middle Ages, it has been translated into more languages than any other writing produced in Latin antiquity except the works of the great poet Virgil.

A Longer Journey Than Expected

The changes in the life of Augustine that *The Confessions* records indicate a hallmark in the history of Western Christianity. These changes reveal how far one has to go and to how great an extent one has to be made new in moving from the culture's dream of perfection and achievement to the church's vision of the holy life. Most of the educated people of Augustine's day thought of Christianity as a simple matter of adding faith to the best ideas and values of the day. Or they thought of faith as a new, sure, and certain starting point, which if followed could bring one to that same vision of the good and the same harmony of self that the philosophy of the day promised. This latter view was what our convert of 387 embraced.

In the year preceding his baptism, Augustine even wrote a treatise titled *The Happy life (De Beata Vita)*, using a phrase that described the happy state of those persons who pursued true learning and true religion. When he was quite old, Augustine took back some of the early optimism of this treatise. However, the young convert fully expected to make up for the lost time he had spent pursuing error by achieving the "happy life" through study, prayer, and good works.

The forty-three-year-old bishop who wrote *The Confessions* was a sadder but wiser Christian person than he was in 387. He had begun to discover that God is in charge of our lives and our learnings. Augustine had begun to discover what some of his contemporaries could never embrace, that the Christian religion is not simply an addition to the best insights of the culture and that we cannot achieve perfection by combining our hard work with a little empowerment from God. Modern converts who have awakened some months or years after the enthusiasm of their first conversion to see a long and troubled Christian life ahead know what happened to Augustine in his first crucial decade as a Christian.

At the time of his conversion Augustine had hoped to see and enjoy the vision and presence of God in the *near* future. But five years before writing *The Confessions*, he wrote in *Expositions on the Psalms* (A.D. 392) that he had begun to worry about how long life's journey can seem: "It is only looking forward to the future which makes this life seem long."[1] By the time of *The Confessions*, Augustine was fully aware that the Christian life was and is a long pilgrimage for which God has given us a pledge but no sustained and final guarantee of success while in this life. Augustine lived by hope, not by achievement; by promise, not by fulfillment. In other words, he lived by faith.

We see the goal of all our living before us, the heavenly Jerusalem. We become aware of God's presence itself; but we only catch glimpses, in hope, in faith. Thus, the mature Christian bishop recorded his chastened and disciplined expectations for the Christian life as a part of the extended love song to God he called *The Confessions*.

Augustine had "settled in" for the long and painful haul of Christian life. Three of the factors that caused such a drastic revision of Augustine's viewpoint are these: (1) Augustine had discovered that Christianity

26

is more about love, specifically our love for God, than it is about our learning and achievement. That fact means that he had begun to struggle with and to comprehend scriptural understandings of God's grace. (2) The discovery of God's grace had begun to undercut Augustine's inflated self-confidence. (3) As a middle-aged person, the reality and implications of death and mortality had touched Augustine personally and entered directly into his thinking. To the first of these discoveries we now turn.

The Student of the Scriptures

The Bible changed Augustine from a thinking lover to a loving thinker. Specifically, the church's hymn book, the Psalms, began to drench him with the language of the church's love and praise. And Paul's writings taught Augustine a way to conceptualize the Christian life in a way that was considerably at odds with the cultural norms of so-called "successful" living.

The very title of Augustine's great spiritual autobiography, *Confessions*, was taken from one of the commonest verbs in the Psalms, "to confess." The word signifies a prayer to God, a confession of one's sin, and, above all, the lifting of one's prayers in praise to God. As John and Charles Wesley knew, what the congregation sings affects Christians deeply. Augustine's study of the Psalms lured him deeper and deeper into biblical ways of speaking and thinking.

The language of the Psalms expressed some of Augustine's deepest experiences as he looked back over his life's journey. When his mother died in the little house in Ostia, Italy (before his return to North Africa), Augustine heard the household filling with the strains of the North African church's funeral hymn, our Psalm 101. When Augustine thought about the fact that a number of his friends and both of his parents were dead and he needed to describe for his hearers the fully adult condition of being shorn of protectors and standing in lonely adulthood, it is to

27

the Psalms that he turned to name God's name, "Father of orphans."[2]

Hundreds of allusions to the Psalms and no less than 180 citations fill *The Confessions*. Above all, the Psalms taught Augustine how to render praise to God; and for Augustine praise was clearly the equivalent of love.

Augustine opened *The Confessions*, his extended love song to God, with these words: "Great thou art, O Lord, and greatly to be praised, great is Thy power and to Thy wisdom there is no limit."[3]

Augustine's study of the Psalms had contributed to the development of a much grander, warmer, and more God-centered world view than the young convert had possessed. The Psalms had emphasized for him not only how our universe must be centered around God and oriented toward the loving praise of our Creator but had also highlighted the impossibility of human beings achieving that awareness unaided by God.

The God of the Psalms is active on our behalf. And because of our sin, we need the God of the Psalms to be active on our behalf in a way and to a degree the young convert had not realized. Augustine's *Expositions on the Psalms* (written in 392) reveals that he had begun to suspect that his old habits and his attachment to sin were more than a passing fault that he could easily overcome. He continued to believe that perfection is attainable in this life, but he was beginning to realize that God must play a far bigger part in perfecting us than Augustine first suspected. So, in commenting on Psalm 6, Augustine noted that the soul is held captive in worldly desires and is powerless to rise from this situation until it is healed:

> But in saying *every night* [Psalm 6:7], the Psalmist wished perhaps to depict a man of good will who perceives a certain amount of the light of truth, but sometimes sinks back into worldly pleasures through the weakness of his flesh. As a result, one is compelled to undergo in mind an alteration

of light and darkness. *With the mind I serve the law of God*, he says, as he rejoices in the daylight; yet he slips back once more into the night with the words, *But with the flesh the law of sin*.[4]

This passage highlights Augustine's increasing awareness that the soul has difficulty breaking out of its old patterns. Paul's letter to the Romans, especially Romans 7, had also begun to influence Augustine's emerging picture of the Christian life. Paul's writings were beginning to enter the heart of what Augustine was attempting, that is, the achievement of Christian perfection.

The Manichaeans had introduced Augustine to Paul (see Chapter 2). When Augustine converted to Christianity, he used against the Manichaeans the very author they had introduced to him. Augustine began his detailed study of Paul for purposes of refuting the Manichaeans.

Augustine, the young convert, believed that the person Paul was describing in Romans 7 (especially in verses 21-25) was a person only beginning to set out on the Christian life. Such a person is torn between wanting to serve God and delighting "in the law of God, in my innermost self" on the one hand but finding in one's "members" that the law of sin still operates (Romans 7:22-23) on the other.

By A.D. 392, however, Augustine had begun to suspect that the internal warfare of the self about which Paul wrote might be a bit longer term. By the time *The Confessions* appeared in 400–401, Augustine had concluded that Paul referred to Paul himself, that the statements in Romans 7 were autobiographical and thus described not a temporary stage of struggle with "the old man" but the true shape of mature Christian living.

Thus, Paul gave Augustine a new pattern for the Christian life, a pattern quite different from classical views. Augustine came to realize that all persons are trapped in persistent patterns of living and are subject to those patterns in ways that prevent persons from breaking permanently free to progress to perfection. The old classical view that the human will needs only right thinking, discipline, and practice to break free of human limitations failed the test of Augustine's experience. He discovered in himself and in Scripture that some habits are so deeply ingrained in the self that they exert a continuous force or a compulsive power. As God's love calls up a new will to love and to obey the commandments, the old will still clings with a frightening tenacity to the practices and deeds that the convert has come to hate.

Augustine realized that even so simple a bad habit as swearing has roots that go deep into the involuntary parts of the self. Thus, the problem is not simply that we do not will to break the bad habit. The problem is that the self cannot pull itself together enough to will the elimination of the habit's force and to will the good.

So, whatever good the mature bishop of *The Confessions* achieved, he now ascribed to God's action for him and in him and not to his own meritorious effort. God's love, God's grace, God's seeking of us and leading us step by step is what will bring us safely home. God is not simply our destination. God is also the very means by which we reach that destination. Hence the Augustine of *The Confessions* was a person who had loosened his grasp on himself and had begun to open his hands to God for help toward a future that Augustine realized he could not control. He was learning to trust in God.

A Changed Self-portrait

The deepening awareness of God's trustworthiness changed Augustine's self-portrait. When Augustine thought about himself apart from God's love and mercy, he was a puzzle even to himself. Augustine wrote, "For in your sight I have become a riddle to myself, and that is my infirmity."[5]

We do not really know ourselves or others. We know that we will be tempted in this life, but we do not know the outcome. In fact, we cannot predict our own emotional behavior with certainty.

Once a young man who was assured that he was in charge of his life and would soon put it right, the middle-aged Augustine shrunk in horror from such a prospect. The bright young convert who set out on the head's journey to understand and to teach truth yielded to the chastened Christian under grace, dependent on God for whatever small understanding of truth he had: "For under the inspiration of none but you [God] do I trust myself to speak the truth, for you are the truth."[6]

Augustine had been brought to one of the most important insights of Christian life: We who seek God are dependent on the very object we are seeking.

The Embodied Self

Augustine had concluded that the self that seeks God is a flawed self that requires a lifetime of healing. The sign of that need of healing is our mortality. This awareness of mortality forms one of the major themes of *The Confessions*. The embodied self remains always a mortal self.

In the first year after Augustine's conversion and while Augustine was on the doorstep of his bright hopes for the future, his beloved seventeen-year-old son, Adeodatus, died. No one who has ever laid a child, parent, dear friend, or relative in the grave can avoid discovering how great a gulf exists between those who are safe with God and we who live yet in this mortal body. In his grief Augustine turned to God: "Father and mother and protectors are absent, yet you are present, you who have created us, who have called us."[7]

Nebridius, one of the close friends of Augustine's youth, converted to Christianity shortly after Augustine did. But Nebridius had also died and Augustine wrote,

There he [Nebridius] lives, in that place of which he asked so many questions of me, a poor,

31

ignorant man. No longer does he put his ear to my mouth, but he puts his spiritual mouth to your fountain, and in accordance with his desire he drinks in wisdom, as much as he can, endlessly happy. Nor do I think that he is so inebriated by that fountain of wisdom as to become forgetful of me, for you, O Lord, of whom he drinks, are mindful of us."[8]

The life of perfection and safety with God vanished, except in glimpses, behind the veil of this mortal life in the body. The full reality of how our mortality enshrines a resistance to its very creator gradually dawned on Augustine.

A forty-year-old person who does not begin to take his or her body seriously is not likely to live very long! And Augustine's age worked on him to force him to give greater attention to the body. His age also coincided with his growing understanding of the Scriptures, especially Romans and Genesis 1–3. He had worked on these passages intermittently throughout this crucial decade of his life. These Scriptures convinced him that mortality is more than a theological idea or a problem that can be reversed and healed by right thinking and right living.

So, Augustine's warmth, intelligence, and his study of the Scriptures prevented him from flogging his body into submission, the ancient equivalent of the health club route. For force and mortification of the body are neither what the Scriptures teach nor what the Christian needs. Healing, not flagellation, is required. The heart is not completely independent; the mind and will are fettered by habit; and the body reveals and preserves the flaws of the self.

Thus, Augustine's ten-year pursuit of perfection and self-control ended, not in victory, but in praise of the Creator and in need of the Savior's continuous healing. When the sadder but wiser Christian took up his pen to struggle with Genesis 1–3 (a struggle that had been going on all through this decade), he was a thoroughly chastened and loving Christian theologian who wrote, "May God, then, who is immutably good, cultivate the good man and guard him. By Him we must be unceasingly made and unceasingly perfected, clinging to Him and remaining turned to Him. . . . For we are His work of art not only in so far as we are human but also in so far as we are good."[9]

Augustine had used the crucial decade of his forties, not to finish his journey, but to begin it again, this time step by step in God's healing care. Augustine had moved from being a philosophical commentator on human perfectibility to being a Christian prayerfully contemplating "holy living and holy dying." His work as a Christian theologian, steeped in the Scriptures, was fully underway.

---

[1] From *St. Augustine on the Psalms*, translated and annotated by Dame Scholastica Hebgin and Dame Felicitas Corrigan (The Newman Press, 1960); Vol. I, page 73.

[2] From *The Confessions of St. Augustine*, translated by John K. Ryan (Image Books, 1960); Book 9, Chapter 12, Section 32.

[3] From *The Confessions*; 1, 1, 1.

[4] From *St. Augustine on the Psalms*; page 68.

[5] From *The Confessions*; 10, 33, 50.

[6] From *The Confessions*; 13, 25, 38.

[7] From *The Confessions*; 9, 8, 18.

[8] From *The Confessions*; 9, 3, 6.

[9] From *St. Augustine: The Literal Meaning of Genesis*, translated and annotated by John Hammond Taylor, S.J., in Ancient Christian Writers Series (Newman Press, 1983); Vol. II, page 51.

4

The Church in the World

If we had ended the story of Augustine's life with the years 400 and 401, we would have done both Augustine and ourselves a quite serious disservice indeed. We would have watched as a middle-aged bishop's personal experience and scriptural growth gradually and gently edged him toward praise and away from pride. We would have seen him in our mind's eye in the midst of the congregation, lifting songs of praise to his Creator in gratitude and harmony.

And then we would have turned our mind's eye to our modern Christian world—crisscrossed with ecumenical bickering, checkered with clerical fraud, and rife with violence done by Christians to Christians. On Sunday morning we might even have looked around our own local congregations at people who were acting and living at cross-purposes with their Christian professions of faith. Thus, we might long to be among those saints of Late Antiquity, shepherded by a great and learned leader of the church and surrounded by true Christians.

But Augustine did not live in a perfect world or time. He lived in the midst of a people and a culture as chaotic as our own. We err seriously if we idealize the past and assume that it was a more perfect time than our own. Augustine knew that it was not. And it was within that world and that culture that Augustine the working pastor, bishop, and ecclesiastical politician had to work out his doctrine of the church. Augustine's doctrine of the church was formed as much by the face-to-face world of real persons as it was by a study of the Scriptures. (And everyone knows that people are much harder to read and understand than books!)

The Church as a Body

To stand in Augustine's congregation on a Sunday morning to chant a psalm was to stand in the midst of a mixed body of folks, as Augustine discovered almost instantly upon becoming a priest. To him, the priesthood in some ways seemed more like a descent than an elevation, a descent into the work-a-day world of parish matters, petty jealousies, and, above all, hidden sins.

Being a Christian in Late Antiquity was both fashionable and even advantageous. In A.D. 399, the Western emperor Honorius issued an edict closing the pagan shrines in North Africa forever. This edict came at the end of a half century of almost unrelieved imperial harrassment of paganism. Thus, many pagans faked conversions, changing nothing about their old ways. So, as a working pastor who had his own flock in mind, Augustine wrote,

How can the just man be directed, then, except in secret? For now that the Christian name has arrived at the zenith of its glory, the very actions people admired in the first stages of Christianity, when worldly powers crushed the saints beneath persecution, do but serve to foster the growth of hypocrisy and pretense in people who are

35

Christian in name but prefer to please humans rather than God. Amidst the confusion of such hypocrisy, how . . . is the just man to be directed except by the God who searches hearts and reins, who looks into our thoughts, here designated by the word "heart" and our pleasures, here called "reins"?[1]

The Augustine who joined the Roman church in the world as a pastor learned that, not only is the church in the world, the world is in the church. Thus, to survey Augustine's preaching over his long pastoral career is to recognize in his sermons quite a depressing list of sins, such as theft, fornication, assault, and even murder!

To chant praises to God in Augustine's church was to rub shoulders with a large number of folks whose lips and whose lives were not going in the same direction. So, Augustine's gradual setting aside of the doctrine of final perfection in this life, which we traced in his personal and scriptural development up to the time of *The Confessions* (see Chapter 3 of this study book), had its church and community parallel during the same time period. Augustine had to give up the notion that the universal church in this world can be exactly identified with the "church of the saints."

The problem was not that God's presence could not be sensed and seen to be at work in the congregation. The problem was how hard it is to tell in whom God is *truly* working. The Augustine who wrote *The Confessions* was a person who had come to the conclusion that only in our hearts are we what we truly are before God. And no one can see the heart but God.

Thus, the judgment of who was in *her or his heart* a true Christian had to wait until God, who sees the innermost motivations, had spoken. Flagrant and notorious sinners could be identified and winnowed out, but only God could see the religion of the "hidden."

Augustine gradually realized that the church is a mixed body of "the wheat and the tares" (Matthew

13:30), saints and sinners, who could not be separated into the pure or "elect" members and the lost until the Last Judgment. Just as the individual cannot be fully perfected while in the body, so the church in history is and must remain a mixed body. Augustine was driven to this doctrine of the church not only by the uneven quality of the lives of his own parishioners but by the presence on his doorstep of another church that actually claimed to be the pure church, the Donatist church.

A Church of the Saints

To stand in Augustine's church building to praise God was to be located so near to the Donatist building that the Donatists' loud worship on occasions drowned out the Roman praises. Augustine was not the only bishop of Hippo Regius in his early years there; and his church, the Roman church throughout the West, was not the only church in Africa. A group called the Donatists embraced approximately half of the North Africans and most of the native highlanders in their communion. This church claimed to be the true church of Africa, the church of the martyrs, and the church of the true saints who had never compromised with the pagan authorities.

Donatist roots went back to the last great persecution of the church by paganism before the conversion of the emperor Constantine in A.D. 312. During these persecutions, a number of Christians had obeyed the imperial orders to sacrifice to the pagan gods; and some clergy had obeyed the command to hand over copies of the Scriptures to the imperial officials.

Many African Christians were horrified that clergy had surrendered the Scriptures and holy objects to imperial officials. These deeds seemed to the people to be like Judas's betrayal when he handed Jesus Christ over to the authorities. Therefore, these Christians vowed never to cooperate with or to receive the sacraments of baptism and Holy Communion from such priests.

Many Christians thought such betrayers were compromised or polluted. So, these Christians thought that the sacraments and the congregations of such priests would be tainted. Many African Christians feared contracting what they thought was a spiritually deadly "disease." They felt that giving in to Rome during the persecutions was an idolatrous pollution whose infection could erase that holiness without which we shall not see the Lord and for which they felt forgiveness was not available. These people were quite firm in their beliefs, to say the least.

Unfortunately, and probably because the urban clergy were afraid of the fanatical Christians of the countryside, a new bishop of Carthage was elected just after the persecution to fill a vacancy in 311. This bishop was elected without the participation of the chief bishop and clergy of Numedia, the highlands of modern Algeria. This election was illegal and had great consequences for the countryside, for the bishop of Carthage had come to be regarded as the spiritual leader of all Africa.

The Numedian bishops were not only insulted, they were horrified! Caecilian, the new bishop, was rumored to have been elected and consecrated by priests who had handed over sacred objects to the pagans in the recent persecution. Fury and fright swept the North African church, and many people completely withdrew from communion with Caecilian and all his church.

Repeated appeals throughout the West and to the new Christian emperor Constantine removed all legal doubt of Caecilian's "taint." But this did not satisfy the new wing of the African church. These people would not cooperate with the judgments of ecclesiastical councils or obey orders from the Christian emperor to reunite with the Roman clergy and to surrender church properties to them. In this confusing situation, the church in Africa urged Constantine to persecute the *Donatists*, as they were now named (after their second leader, Donatus).

A brief persecution followed. Some Donatists were

killed, and the schism solidified. The Donatists began to claim that they were not only the church that was loyal to the martyrs but that they *were now themselves the church of the martyrs*.

The success of the Donatists among the native peoples of North Africa was extensive. The Donatists claimed to be the true church of Africa, following most closely the long traditions of the church of Africa. They felt that they alone respected and represented the "expensive grace" of true martyr Christianity. They considered themselves the true sons and daughters of the most beloved and famous martyr-bishop of all North African history, Cyprian. And like Cyprian, they saw their church as the "walled garden" of Paradise, the church of the pure. Also like Cyprian, the Donatists practiced rebaptism of Christians who came to their churches from other communions.

A Church of the Spirit

Basing their arguments on the writings of their great third-century saint, Cyprian, the Donatists argued that "tainted" churches dispense invalid sacraments. Donatists said that the automatic converting power of a sacrament like baptism is not present because the Holy Spirit is not present in a tainted church. The Donatists said that their sacraments, unlike those of their competitors, retained the divine power of the Holy Spirit.

Roman Christians of North Africa had a separate idea about precisely what spirit possessed the Donatists. Beginning in the mid-fourth century, partisans of the Donatist church grew increasingly violent in the countryside. Gangs of them wandered about the unpoliced rural areas, falling with their clubs upon hapless Roman officials or Roman Christian bishops and clergy. Violence and intimidation, as well as great devotion to matters of sanctity, checkered the Donatist movement.

Augustine's Response to Donatism

From the early 390's, Augustine had been engaged in refuting Donatism. But beginning in 400, he turned to refuting Donatism with increased seriousness by publishing a treatise titled *On Baptism Against the Donatists*. In this work he argued what were and what became the Western church's views of the ministry and the sacraments.

According to Augustine, what makes the church truly the church is its universality, its unbroken communion across time and distance. The true church is not shut up and confined in any one nation and has never compromised its grace of charity by breaking fellowship with the church universal. If the Donatists wanted to model themselves after Cyprian, wrote Augustine, then they should model his charity for other Christians. Cyprian was no schismatic! When Cyprian had differences with other communions, Augustine argued (not, by the way, with historical accuracy), the peace of charity prevailed. The guarantee of the purity of the church is its unity.

Baptism is Christ's to dispense, not any mortal human's. Since Christ grants the baptism, the moral quality of the priest who administers the sacrament has nothing to do with the spiritual efficacy of the event.

How then does the true sacrament operate? Augustine made a distinction between the sacrament and its work in the believer. If the intention of the believer is not right, the sacrament simply does not work for the salvation of the person. Augustine had seen too many cases of insincere conversions and perfunctory baptisms to hold Donatist opinions on how the sacrament worked. In the mixed "wheat and tares" world of the church, even baptism is no guarantee of salvation. Only God's working of faith and obedience in human hearts will determine one's salvation, not the "purity" of the person who administers a sacrament or the purity of the one who receives it. When God gives faith to the recipient, then and only then does grace operate for salvation. That happens, Augustine believed, only in communion with the Roman church.

How then could one of the greatest leaders of the African church, Cyprian, have taught and practiced a wrong doctrine, namely, that people who came to the church from other communions must be rebaptized? Cyprian was simply *wrong*, Augustine said. Cyprian's place in heaven and his high position in our esteem does not rest in his infallibility. He was human like the rest of us. The love of God is what saves us, not our knowledge. It is the orientation of our heart that saves, not the exactitude of our opinions.

No one knew better than Augustine how uncertain the foundation for salvation could be if it rested on the infallibility and purity of human beings. Augustine had his own life as a case in point and could counsel others publicly from his own example:

> Augustine is a bishop of the Catholic Church. He carries his own burden and will one day have to render to God an account of it. I know that he clings to the company of the good. If he is himself evil, then he will know it; yet even if he is good, it is not to him that I cling, for in the Catholic Church I have learned, above all things, never to make a man the foundation of my trust.[2]

This quotation, from a sermon originally preached at Carthage in 403, shows us Augustine's best argument against Donatist views of holiness. But in general the years after 400 show us a more unattractive silhouette of Augustine, for he turned in earnest to eliminate the schism. And as he did so, he turned increasingly to the force and power of the state to aid him in this venture, especially in the years 405–411.

A Shadow on the Religion of the Heart

By the opening years of the fifth century, Augustine had increasingly emphasized the hidden work of God in human hearts as the source of true conversion and salvation. Such a conclusion could have led Augustine logically to a doctrine of toleration, since only God can work such a deep change in hearts.

Alas for the West, Augustine went, also logically, in the opposite direction. If the work of salvation belongs to God, then why not restore people to the church whether they want to be restored or not and let God work out their salvation? Our task is to compel and God's task is to convert, thought Augustine.

Thus, Augustine became an advocate of compelling the Donatists to come in. The theologian of the heart became the theoretician of the just use of force to unify the church and to purge it of dangerous elements. The bishop of Hippo ignored complaints by the Donatists that the true church was a persecuted church, not a persecuting church.

Historians of Christianity have argued deftly and accurately that Augustine arrived at his position for a number of good reasons. The Donatists had become increasingly violent and dangerous in the explosive atmosphere of imperial and aristocratic misrule. Some Donatists even backed a revolt against Rome by Gildo, the count of Africa, in 399. Roman clergy and laity suffered regular violence at the hands of Donatists. And when Augustine and the Roman clergy were able to bring the schismatic Donatists under imperial laws outlawing heretics, one Donatist bishop locked himself and his entire congregation in his church and threatened to burn the entire congregation alive rather than surrender his church and people to Roman Christianity.

Some scholars have argued that the Donatist controversy represented Augustine's re-Africaniza-tion, his settling into a tougher world of ecclesiastical politics in North Africa than his school books and his rearing in an entirely Romanized town like Thagaste had prepared him to face. And, above all, historians point to something quite puzzling to modern people committed to tolerance: Augustine and his contemporaries claimed to discover that force sometimes worked. A number of people compelled to become Roman Christians became in fact grateful and productive Christians, thanks to God's invisible grace!

All this background information helps explain why, in additon to debate, discussion, pleading, and preaching, the church added force as a means of trying to eliminate the schism. But these reasons are not finally satisfying. With the wisdom of hindsight and the luxury of religious freedom, we can see that such a position was simply wrong and that what it set loose as a biblically based precedent in history was simply atrocious. A shadow lies across the religion of the heart. How shall we regard this shadow?

Here we must humbly acknowledge about Augustine what he himself had concluded about Cyprian. Augustine was wrong, though we must not prefer our heart to his. He lives now with God. Now free of the mortal body, perhaps he, like Cyprian, sees with greater clarity that truth to which his charity made him so worthy to attain. For we, the contemporary church in the world, have every right to decide on a proper course of action but no right at all to judge the hearts of those who have chosen wrongly.

---

[1]From *St. Augustine on the Psalms*, translated and annotated by Dame Scholastica Hebgin and Dame Felicitas Corrigan (The Newman Press, 1960); Vol. I, pages 85–86.

[2]From *Expositions on the Psalms*, by Augustine, quoted in *Augustine the Bishop*, translated by Brian Battershaw and G. R. Lamb (Sheed and Ward, 1961); pages 112–13.

5

The Final Journey Into Grace

By the year 412, the struggle with Donatism was winding down. Augustine was fifty-eight years old and on the threshold of the period in his life that modern developmentalists call late adulthood. As we contemporary Christians are beginning to notice, we are growing older both as an American population and as members of mainline denominations. We are churches of older members set within an aging population.

We need to pay some attention to Augustine as an older adult, for he focuses for us the promise and the problem of this age bracket. On the one hand, older adults are generally confident of themselves as Christians and have a richness of experience to impart. On the other hand, age creates the possibility of falling dangerously out of touch with our younger contemporaries and of equating an older generation's conclusions and discoveries with the very heart of the Christian faith itself.

Augustine's advancing age and his great influence exactly coincided with the Pelagian controversy, named after Pelagius, the movement's most articulate spokesperson. The controversy mushroomed into an exploration by Christian thinkers into the limits of human freedom and into the exact horizons of human possibility in the work of human salvation. The question put in its bluntest form is, "How much does God do in saving us and how much do we ourselves do with God's help?"

The Older Adult Augustine

The Augustine of the years 411–430 was the aging Augustine who showed many of the blessings and problems associated with late adulthood. On the one hand, this time in his life was the period of Augustine's richest and fullest genius. In these years he wrote his greatest treatises on God's grace and gave to Christian history one of its most enduring classics, *The City of God*. In these years he brought a matchless and mature Christian experience to the great issues of Scripture and salvation, sanctity and ethics. Augustine now knew by having lived and by having tried out things.

On the other hand, Augustine found his own "voice" in a unique way. He was no longer particularly concerned about what others thought of him, and he was too famous to tolerate much interference with his opinions. He increasingly came to identify his own informed experience with the doctrine of the universal church. In fact, Augustine's unique genius was carrying him deeper into his own lines of thinking and further from those of his contemporaries.

Pelagius's Thought

Ironically, Augustine found as one of his greatest enemies a man whose own mature thought resembled that of Augustine's positions as a young person. Like Augustine, Pelagius was an ascetic Christian intellectual, well-read in the classics and deeply committed to perfection in the Christian life. He had been a resident of the city of Rome and lectured on Paul to a circle of Christian aristocrats in the mid-390's exactly at the same time that Augustine was working on Paul in

North Africa. But here Pelagius and Augustine definitely part company.

Augustine's life and study had led him by the time of *The Confessions* to emphasize the Christian's dependence on God's grace for knowing and performing the good. However, in contrast, Pelagius resembled in his mature thinking what Augustine had thought quite early in his life, namely, that God had endowed human nature with the capacity to perform the good and to obey the commandments. Pelagius was interested in encouraging persons on to the venture Augustine had abandoned by the time of *The Confessions*. That venture was the achievement of the holy life based on using the capacities that God has given us. So Pelagius wrote,

> When I have to discuss the principles of right conduct and the leading of a holy life, I usually begin by showing the strength and characteristics of human nature. By explaining what it can accomplish, I encourage the soul of my hearer to different virtues. To call a person to something he considers impossible does him no good. . . . Despair of success will kill every effort to acquire the impossible. . . . With a lower estimation of its capacity, a soul will be less diligent and insistent in pursuing virtue.[1]

Pelagius went on in this letter to emphasize the goodness of God in giving each person reason and judgment so that by our own wills we can accomplish God's will. And Pelagius used many examples of heroic performances by persons in the Bible to illustrate his point, including Abel, Abraham, Isaac, Jacob, and Job.

Pelagius's path lay quite close to the one that Augustine as a new Christian convert had trod. But as we saw, Augustine broke with classical doctrines of human perfectibility by the time of *The Confessions*. The Augustine of *The Confessions* was a person who emphasized the enduring power of sin and the constant need of receiving God's grace. Thus, he wrote in prayer to God, "Give what you command and command what you will."[2]

When a bishop read this passage of *The Confessions* to Pelagius (likely Paulinus of Nola), Pelagius is said to have burst into a fit of anger over it. This approach was precisely the kind of doctrine that Pelagius and the people in his circle believed would undercut their movement by de-emphasizing the free will of persons, overemphasizing the sin-filled helplessness of persons, and paralyzing the grace-assisted person's progress to perfection. Many Christians shared Pelagius's view of the Scriptures as a book teaching that free will leads with God's help to moral perfection. In fact, this understanding was the most representative view of Christian thinkers in the whole Eastern half of the Empire (Mediterranean Christians from Constantinople [Istanbul] to Palestine).

Augustine had heard rumors about the teaching of Pelagianism, but matters came to a head when Pelagius's disciple Caelestius was arraigned at Carthage on some specific charges of heresy. Caelestius was charged with teaching that Adam's fall did not cause human death (Adam, he thought, was always mortal) and that infants do not sin and hence do not require baptism. In short, Caelestius maintained that people could keep the commandments sinlessly because Adam's fall did not damage the human race as a whole. A fight was on that would occupy Augustine to the end of his life.

Before the Pelagian controversy was over, it involved Christians in councils in North Africa, in Palestine, and in Italy. In 417, Pope Innocent I, bishop of Rome, condemned Pelagian doctrines in his capacity as judge of the ecclesiastical "last court of appeals" in the West. When Innocent died that same year, the new pope, Zosimus, an Easterner and so more sympathetic to the Pelagians, reopened the case. However, the emperor, Honorius, fearing riots in Rome over the issue, condemned and expelled the Pelagians from the city. The Africans also held a synod that firmly condemned Pelagian views. This contro-versy called forth and crystallized everything Augus-tine had been thinking about sin and salvation.

Augustine's Position

Augustine believed Adam's fall left each of us a legacy of mortality and guilt. With a North African's love of family genealogy, Augustine concluded that all of us since Adam are biologically related. Only Adam and Eve were created directly by God; the rest of us were created by human procreation. Thus, when Adam sinned against God by evil desire, he passed that sin down the family tree.

In short, Augustine believed that Adam physically transmitted his sin to us. Thus, the late Augustine increasingly saw human beings as a "lump of perdition," that is, constituted out of and found in one sinful human nature.

Furthermore, Augustine was not able to think about death as anything but a just punishment for our sins. He believed that death was not natural. Augustine thought that death was a terrible punish-ment for our turning away from our Creator, our highest good, our only hope. Here the older man took one more step deeper into the psychology of death and dying.

Augustine on Love

Even more important to the formation of Augus-tine's thought was the rising position grace had come to hold for him. When Augustine spoke of "the love of God," he almost always meant *our love for God*. This is the love that God commands us to have; and when we have it, we are both safe and able to love ourselves and our neighbors.

By 400, Augustine had realized that we cannot love someone who has not appeared to us. Thus, God must choose us, call us, and appear to us in order for us to love God. God must first make the divine self available to us. Thus, *The Confessions* showed a mild predestination. God chooses to call and empower some persons to love God. Like all ancient theorists of love, Augustine knew that this process on the person's part was both an intellectual decision to love one worthy of admiration and an emotional decision to prefer and to cling to the object of his or her love.

However, Augustine came to believe that human beings cannot control this decision of what to love and obey ultimately. From his liturgical life and in his exegesis, what Augustine came to see was that God does not command the performance of the commandments, the "keeping" of them; but God commands the fulfillment of them by our freely given love. It is not the "letter" of the commandments but the "spirit" that we are to seek. It is not love but *perfect love* that we must achieve, best represented by the complete and harmonious inner delight in God's commandments. Such a complete inner assent is almost impossible to achieve in human life.

Augustine as an older adult was a person who knew that people do not pass through and thus beyond sin. And at precisely this point in his thought, Augustine had to be most careful not to arouse the anger of the great and holy ascetics of his day. These ascetics expected to pass on to perfection, and the way Augustine carefully skirted this issue in a letter he wrote to Paulinius of Tyre revealed Augustine's concern not to arouse them.

However, Augustine had passed beyond his contemporaries' understandings of sin; and his doctrine of grace began to take hold. Augustine discovered a fundamental fault in the self that continued to serve sin unless God changed the heart and gave persons the wellsprings of delight in or preference for God. For Augustine, these wellsprings of delight, the overwhelming preference for loving God, came increasingly to signify God's work in our hearts. The *capacity* to believe and to love may belong to the natural human self, but the actual *believing and the loving* belong to grace.

Reinterpreting Paul Once Again

In the 390's, Augustine had been at work on Paul's letter to the Romans and had twice failed to crack open its meaning in any systematic way. His early work on Romans showed that Augustine did not understand how Paul's language about grace related to the language about love. In the course of his late develoment, Augustine came to see more clearly than ever before that the love the gospel commands is identical to the grace that Paul said God gives to believers. Thus, Augustine wrote in commenting on Romans and Psalm 31:19, "In this manner it is that the great abundance of His [God's] sweetness,—that is, the law of faith,—His love which is in our hearts, and shed abroad, is perfected in them that hope in Him, that good may be wrought by the soul, healed not by the fear of punishment, but by the love of righteousness."[3]

In this way all the love in our hearts by which we are made fit for God is *given* by God. This love is meritorious for our salvation in that God is the source. God gives this love to us freely without our deserving it, and we are freely to respond to it. But salvation is entirely the work of God—from our first calling, through the aiding of our response, to the fulfillment and perfection of our love, and our perseverance in love to the end.

Augustine had tried to preserve some measure of human merit, initiative, or cooperation in his doctrine of grace. As a younger man, he had insisted upon it. In fact, the Pelagians used his earlier positions against him. Augustine responded that the Pelagians failed to track his later progress on grace. He now fully understood the words of Paul in 1 Corinthians 4:7b, "What have you that you did not receive?" In one of his latest treatises, written in 429, Augustine said that he tried to preserve a doctrine of free will. However, God's grace overcame him.

The old Augustine knew that God provides every motivation necessary for salvation. More important,

Augustine knew exactly what most persons do not know, that is, that no one knows why God chooses, aids, and perfects some people and not others. All persons share in and add to Adam's fault. God predestines some people to enter God's select company of "the elect," Augustine believed. God not only chooses them and sanctifies them but grants these people the gift of perseverance. All we can say about why God saves some and not others, wrote Augustine, is that the reasons are hidden in the judgments of God. Augustine thought that we can learn from Paul only that humans are humbled that God may be exalted.

Thus, infant baptism rose in importance for the late Augustine as the sign of God's choosing us before we can know God. Just as the church claims infants in baptism before they know and merit it, so God seeks out the elect. Infant baptism became a metaphor of Augustine's new doctrine of predestination.

The Last Ten Years

Around 420, a young Sicilian, Julian of Eclanum, who resigned his episcopacy over the ascendance of Augustinian views, took up the battle against the grand old man. The warfare in writing that the two men waged against each other (the one from the aristocratic optimism of youth, the other from the hardened pessimism of age) won neither person any awards in history for intellectual sportsmanship. Julian went for the older man's deepest wound, his former association with the Manichaeans. All of Africa, Julian trumpeted, was in the hands of a "Manichaean brigand." He meant Augustine! Augustine, Julian maintained, resurrected the old Manichaean disparagement of creation and creation's God, taught moral paralysis in the ethical life, and demeaned human infancy and human sexuality by dwelling on human corruption.

Augustine responded in a stream of counterarguments that underlined the problematic and corrupt nature of all human activity, especially procreation, and brushed aside his young opponent's arguments in a cursory and insulting way.

Julian's fate was sealed by the great and beloved bishop's learning and contempt. The man who once wrote at length of Cyprian's charity, especially charity for fellow bishops, crammed his intellectual fist down the young Julian's throat. Julian ended his days, not reconciled to the church as a bishop, but as a teacher of secular literature to little children in an obscure Italian village. And Augustine was still berating Julian when the final fever took Augustine to his death in 430.

The Outcome of the Controversy

Augustine won the battle but not the war. He had forged a convincing chain of biblical and historical witnesses for his own day, but his more extreme views on predestination did not pass into the mainline thought of the Middle Ages.

The Council of Orange in 529 transmitted Augustine's view of the effect of Adam's fall on us, the necessity of baptism for salvation, and the unmerited grace of God as the source of our goodness. But the Council of Orange passed quietly over the doctrine of God's arbitrary election and predestination, which Augustine had worked out so carefully. This doctrine and its corollaries were awakened only occasionally before the Reformation. Then during the Reformation, hard-line Augustinianism arose in a quite different manner and setting to soothe or to trouble Christians from the sixteenth through the eighteenth centuries.

An Image of the Controversy

The older Augustine was a man who knew himself to be truly loving toward God and, hence, to be truly loved by God. A person who does not let go of self in loving cannot understand what propelled Augustine toward the elimination of all human claims on salvation. But Augustine was a lover, a lover who credited the beloved with miraculous endowments and powers. And for this reminder Christian history owes Augustine a great debt.

However, Augustine's doctrine of love, especially with regard to perseverance in love to the end, was also forged by a world-weary old pastor who had seen too many human ventures come to naught, too much human promise destroyed or broken, too many professing Christians who were frauds, and too many nice people who were cold of heart and stingy of spirit. If God alone could give, supply, and judge our hearts, that is, judge us where we are most ourselves, how could we ever know who would get safely through this life as a true Christian to the end?

The young Augustine was a Christian setting out on an unsinkable venture, like the R.M.S. *Titanic*. The old pastor was a man whose ship has struck the invisible and hidden purposes of God. As his ship sank, so did his confidence in humans to engineer a safe passage. Pelagius and Julian seemed to him to be men staggering around the slanting deck, assuring folks that all was well, while Augustine, hoping for a lifeboat, sang "Nearer, My God, to Thee." Thus, youth cheered on the saving of the ship and age the letting go.

---

[1]From *Theological Anthropology*, translated and edited by J. Patout Burns (Fortress Press, 1981); pages 40–41.

[2]From *The Confessions of St. Augustine*, translated by John K. Ryan (Image Books, 1960); Book 10, Chapter 29, Section 40.

[3]From *Saint Augustin: Anti-Pelagian Writings*, Vol. V in A Select Library of the Nicene and Post-Nicene Fathers of the Christian Church, edited by Philip Schaff (Wm. B. Eerdmans Publishing Company, 1956); pages 104–105.

6

The Citizen of a Heavenly City

Some individuals and some periods of history are not granted a peaceful old age. Once again, Augustine's fate and that of his culture were intertwined.

The sack of Rome brought Pelagius and Caelestius to North Africa, so Augustine was embroiled in controversy with them until the end of his life. The fall of Rome that brought the Pelagians to Augustine's full notice preoccupied Augustine and resulted in his *The City of God*, written and published serially from the years 413 to 426.

The Pelagian travelers, like so many others who passed over to North Africa or through it, were refugees from the chaotic aftermath of the fall of the West's greatest city. Rome pulled herself together after the sack by Alaric in 410, but the aftershocks would continue for many years. The peace of the city, which really meant the security and safety of the city, was ended. The days of the Early Empire, during which the people of the unwalled city could boast that Rome's legions were her walls, had yielded under the pressure of barbarians on the frontiers to the construction of the Aurelian wall of the late third century. In the early fifth century, neither Rome's legions nor her walls could save the city from Alaric and his Goths.

The Goths were one of a series of Germanic peoples moving west and south toward the Mediterranean region of Europe because other Germanic and Mongol tribes had pushed them in this direction. The Goths appeared in considerable force after A.D. 250 along the Western frontiers of the Roman Empire. By the late fourth century, they had been converted to an Arian brand of Christianity. Ulphilas the Goth, an Arian sympathizer, had translated the Scriptures into the Gothic language. Thus, to Christians of the Empire the Goths were neither Roman nor were they orthodox. The Goths strongly denied the doctrine that Christ was of the same essence as God, coequal Son of the Father. This doctrine had been taught by the Creed of the Council of Nicaea (A.D. 325) to which all orthodox Christians of the Empire, including Augustine, adhered.

The fall of Rome seems to have affected Augustine deeply. Jerome, the great translator of the Latin version of the Bible known as the Vulgate, was also quite disturbed by that event. Even though he was safe in Jerusalem when Rome fell, Jerome felt that the whole world had perished with Rome. But in fact, antiquity continued much as it had, especially in the Greek-speaking East. In the East the sack of Rome rated only two small paragraphs in the best ecclesiastical histories written in the next century.

Nevertheless, like a true pastor, Augustine pushed aside his personal concerns and was preoccupied with his own region and with his own parish and with winding down the Donatist controversy and heating up the Pelagian controversy. His parish was his world! And most probably, Augustine had concluded already in 410 what he would write a decade later in the last book of his *City of God*: "The City of God means salvation [*salvus*], not safety [*salus*]."[1] The middle-aged bishop of *The Confessions*, who had already concluded that this life was a long pilgrimage, an extended journey home to God who is our only safety

55

and security, was not likely to be startled as an older adult when refugees began to stream through his diocese.

Integrity in the Face of Despair

However, when Marcellinus, the imperial commissioner who had been sent to Africa by the emperor to deal with the Donatists, appealed to Augustine, the great bishop snapped to in a huge task. Marcellinus, a devout Christian, was trying to convert the count of Africa, Volusianus, but was making no headway at all. For Volusianus, like other educated pagans, blamed the sack of Rome on Rome's conversion to Christianity. Only one hundred years had elapsed since the first Christian emperor took the throne, and only a decade had passed since many of the pagan shrines had been closed by imperial order. Just as Rome abandoned the old gods that had protected her for over one thousand years for the upstart new religion of Christianity, the city fell, critics said. Could Augustine, Marcellinus wanted to know, furnish proof that such charges were a lie?

So, Augustine went to war again, this time with the entire history of human empire and citizenship. In what came to be seen as one of the most exhaustive treatments of the shape and scope of the meaning of human history ever attempted, Augustine laid out and expanded a view he had arrived at earlier. He told the story of two opposing cities running all through history, one the heavenly, the other the earthly. One was the city of God, and the other the human city (or the city of the devil).

Augustine's *City of God*, encompassing twenty-two books before it was finished, is one of the most enduring classics of antiquity. A lifetime of study and all his intellectual and personal development went into it. *The City of God* is a gold mine of so many things, including classical references, biblical exegesis, theories of statecraft and politics, the history of philosophy, and the Latin language. But for our purposes here, *The City of God* is a gold mine for Augustine's profound understanding of the religion of the heart.

In *The City of God* this aspect of Augustine's thinking, this religion of the heart, comes to its fullest development, perfectly wedded to one of the great tasks of old age. That task involves coming to terms with the full injustice of life and to an awareness of the scope of human destructiveness without losing the capacity to love others and to sense that life has a meaningful direction.

Augustine set as his task the examination of every horror story human history had ever produced. He wanted to prove, first of all, that calamity in the world was not the result of Christianity. Instead, he claimed that here and there one could actually see some relief given by Christianity to what had been an almost unrelieved struggle of the human race since Satan's tumble from heaven and Adam's fall.

The Sorrow of Humanity

Augustine's picture of human life, viewed apart from God's love and purpose, is chilling. He moves from the birth of human society in fratricide with the murder of Abel by Cain, through the relentless domination of one human being by another and one people or nation by another, right straight through to the rape of Christian virgins by the Goths during the sack of Rome.

Augustine turned to a famous rape in pagan Roman history, the rape of Lucretia, as part of his general plan to prove how troubled was Rome's history even before Christian times and as an example of what he considered to be the virtue of pagans. Raped and assaulted, Lucretia told her avenging husband and brother about what had occurred. Then she killed herself from shame over what had happened to her. This way of action was typical of pagan virtues. Augustine did not think of these acts as virtues to be emulated but as "splendid vices," since they had the same self-indulgent and misplaced ends as Roman society. Augustine counseled Christian virgins: Don't be a fool and kill yourself if you've been raped. The issues of this terrible life of ours are not suicide or sanctity. You know your own hearts. If you didn't will or want it, you are not defiled and have no cause whatsoever for shame or guilt.

In *The City of God* rape is a dramatic image of the human situation. Terrible things happen to good people in history, and our sanctity depends not on what happens to us but on the mercy of God who knows and sees our hearts.

Thus, the reader is warned at the outset of *The City of God* that this is not a pleasant book. At least in part, it is as much a catalogue of human pain as it is a catalogue of human politics: "Let every one, then, who thinks with pain on all these great evils, so horrible, so ruthless, acknowledge that this is misery. And if any one either endures or thinks of them without mental pain, this is a more miserable plight still, for he thinks himself happy because he has lost human feeling."[2]

As did Edward Gibbon (the great historian), Augustine as an older adult found the study of history a melancholy task. Even human love, our one great solace in this earthly life, is problematic. Since no one but God sees the heart of another fully, we mistake friends for enemies and enemies for friends. Even those we truly love are an added care because we fear for how they will fare in this life. The dearer and deeper our love for others and the wider our attachments, the more profound our fears for other people become.

Cities of the Heart

It is characteristic of this theologian of the heart—the bishop whom painters depicted as holding out his heart—that he thought the problems and horrors of this life result from the problems of the heart. Thus, after the great catalogue of human vices in *The City of God*, Augustine adds, "These are indeed the crimes of wicked men, yet they spring from that root of error and misplaced love which is born of every son of Adam."[3]

Misplaced love—At the end of his life as at his conversion, the orientation of the heart was still the key, according to Augustine. The orientation of the heart signifies the commitment of the total self in its most characteristic guise. And it is what the heart loves, its orientation, that best places human beings into their truest social groupings and into the heavenly or into the earthly city.

Ancient theorists had debated for centuries about what differentiates a people from a mob or from a random collection of individuals. The ancient theorists generally agreed that a people, a society, or a city (that is, the city viewed from the standpoint of its inhabitants, in accordance with the word's meaning in *The City of God*) differs from a mob in that a people has an organizing principle that orders it. But ancient political thinkers debated and disagreed about exactly what that organizing principle was. In the early books of *The City of God* (written 412–415), Augustine argued about the guesses of classical pagan theorists. But by the latest books, he had found his own Christian voice. According to Augustine, what a people *loves* is the organizing principle for rational human association.

Thus, the story of history is a story of two peoples, two cities, differing from each other in what they love. The earthly city has always loved itself instead of its Creator. It has loved the serving of its own ends, the preservation of its own existence, and its own pride, glory, and earthly victory. Consequently, the earthly city is involved in constant warfare to preserve its fragile peace and to dominate others.

Love and Ends

We are carried to the ends or goals we love. Picking up an image he formulated as a younger man, the old bishop insisted, "The specific gravity of a body is, as it were, its love, whether it tends upward by its lightness or downward by its weight. For, a body is borne by gravity as a spirit is by love, whichever way it is moved."[4]

This statement summarizes Augustine's "law of gravity." We are lifted up by love of our Creator and Savior or cast down and turned in upon ourselves by love of an inferior and evil end.

The City of God

There is a counterweight to the human city weighed down by its love of self. There has always been in history another society (a people, a city) whose love is of God and whose people love one another and all things in God. Born of Abel, not of Cain, these are the people throughout all time who belong to "the perfectly ordered and harmonious communion of those who find their joy in God and one another in God."[5]

The city of God is that body of people that lives by confessing its sins, struggling against lust and domination, and ascribing praise to its Creator for the beauties and sweetness of this life. For this life, which can be so harmful, has been graced with all manner of good and useful solace for our use. But our final enjoyment of all these goods lies only in God and in relation to that blessed city of heaven to which we still belong only fully and finally at the end of this life. If the supreme virtue of the human city is "rule" or "domination," the supreme virtue of the city of God is its humility.

Is the Church the City of God?

By the end of the Donatist controversy, Augustine could not equate the city of God exactly with the earthly church in the world. The visible church was a mixed body. Wheat and tares grow side by side, and members of the city of God suffer with and from other Christians while in this life.

In this unfriendly world, in evil days like these, the Church through the lowliness she now endures is winning the sublime station she is to have in heaven. Meanwhile, the sting of fears and ache of tears, the vexatious toil and hazardous temptations, teach her to rejoice only in the healthy joy of hope. With so many sinners mingled with the saints, all caught in the single fishing net the Gospel mentions, this life on earth is like a sea in which good and bad fishes caught in a net swim about indistinguishably until the net is beached, and the bad ones are separated from the good.[6]

The citizens of the heavenly city are therefore contained in the church in history, and only at the end of history will they be separated out.

Out of the full solemnity of the darkness of this life and the hiddenness of God's purpose in the calling of the elect and in the perseverance of the saints, the city of God rises before Augustine's eyes, spreading before it healing miracles. The power of the saints, the narrative of whose healing stories almost threatens to swamp Book 22 of *The City of God*, entered Augustine's later thinking. In the power of one glorious healing-miracle after another, Augustine saw the foretaste in history of that central miracle of Christian faith: the resurrection of the total self, transformed body and transformed soul. In this marvelous condition the members of the city of God will live eternally with God in heaven, all praising and all loving God. God will be "the object of our unending vision, of our unlessening love, of our unwearying praise."[7] In the heavenly life the freedom not to sin, given by grace in this life, will become "an inability to sin."[8]

A Hierarchical Heaven

Before Augustine's eyes the great pyramid of heaven arose:

But, now, who can imagine, let alone describe,

the ranks upon ranks of rewarded saints, to be graded, undoubtedly, according to their variously merited honor and glory. Yet, there will be no envy of the lower for the higher, as there is no envy of angel for archangel—for this is one of the great blessednesses of this blessed City. The less rewarded will be linked in perfect peace with the more highly favored, but lower could not more long for higher than a finger, in the ordered integration of a body, could want to be an eye. The less endowed will have the high endowment of longing for nothing loftier than their lower gifts.[9]

This quotation shows at one glance both the timelessness and the "time-boundness" of Augustine's vision. Years of praising God and in the love of God helped Augustine break through to a Christian definition of what makes a society most truly a "people" and what makes an individual most truly himself or herself: the focus of his or her love on God, the source and supplier of all that he or she is and has.

At the same time, Augustine's picture of heaven, with its graded hierarchy and its ordered content, shows us how much he belonged to his own time. Augustine's heaven is a very Roman heaven. Augustine's legacy to the Middle Ages stimulated a belief that *order* always comes from God, so order is to be preferred to disorder. Augustine also suggested an aristocratic rather than an egalitarian model for human perfection. Both ideas were products of Roman thinkers.

In the sixth century, Benedict wrote a famous monastic *Rule*. This rule became the basic document for defining social sanctity and the life of perfection in the West. Benedict's *Rule* for monks who wished to live the heavenly life on earth was fully in line with Augustine's picture of heaven. The *Rule* included a graded hierarchy of monks ranked by the order in which they joined the monastery, their wills bound to that of a moral and political "superior" who rules them. If such monks followed the *Rule* all their lives, the *Rule* implied, they would arrive at the apex of the holy pyramid: "the height of humility." Augustine would have been cheered to have read such a very Western and very Roman solution to the Christian problem of social perfection.

Pilgrim Power

Yet, even with such failings, few documents in the West have ever brought such comfort and such delight to Christians living through the pain of radical transition as *The City of God*. Persons passing from one culture, governmental structure, or country to another or persons preparing to depart from this life to the next all have found comfort in its pages. Augustine's *City of God* enshrines a pilgrim's theology for both an entire society in history and for an individual life. It teaches a doctrine of "pilgrim power" by looking squarely at how hard and how hopeless life in this body can be. In love and in confidence, *The City of God* cheers us on our way through, not around, awful and frightening times. It reminds us constantly of our Creator's gifts and our Savior's mercies. By these alone all true pilgrims live.

One example of *The City of God's* impact may suffice. The Christian emperor Charlemagne (A.D. 768–814) was a warrior king who carved a kingdom of temporary stability, peace, and learning out of that very chaotic period that historians used to call "the Dark Ages." Charlemagne learned Latin as a younger man. One of his favorite authors was Augustine. *The City of God* was his favorite book. Rumor reports that in the last few years of his life, Charlemagne wearied of hunting and war, the traditional sports of Frankish kings. Instead, he liked to stay at home reading Augustine's *City of God*. Charlemagne's interest in Augustine was a case of one world-weary older adult reading another across a gulf of time and language Augustine could never have foreseen.

We might suppose Charlemagne read for healing

and for peace of soul. We shall never know whether he found in Augustine that integrity of life that he sought as he prepared to surrender power to the next generation. Neither do we know whether he found there the cleansing power for his bloodstained hands; Charlemagne had lived that "mixed" life of "necessity" in the world of which Augustine wrote so well. But there is certainly love and intellect enough in *The City of God* to have brought Charlemagne both healing and peace of soul. And it is for these qualities above all, whatever Augustine's failings, that the church has revered and remembered and reread Augustine in every age up to the present day.

---

[1]From *The City of God*, translated by Marcus Dods (Edinburgh, 1921); Book 23, Chapter 6.

[2]From *The City of God*; Book 19, Chapter 7.

[3]From *The City of God*; Book 22, Chapter 22.

[4]From *Saint Augustine: The City of God*, translated by Gerald C. Walsh, S. J. and Grace Monahan, O.S.U. (Fathers of the Church, Inc., 1952); Book 11, Chapter 28.

[5]From *Saint Augustine: The City of God*; Book 19, Chapter 17.

[6]From *Saint Augustine: The City of God*; Book 18, Chapter 49.

[7]From *Saint Augustine: The City of God*; Book 22, Chapter 30.

[8]From *Saint Augustine: The City of God*; Book 22, Chapter 30.

[9]From *Saint Augustine: The City of God*; Book 22, Chapter 30.